AWS Organizations SCP Enforcement Troubleshooting

Table of Contents

Chapter 1. Introduction

In the realm of cloud computing, complexity frequently finds its home, especially when it comes to managing multi-account structures within AWS Organizations. From this convolution emerges the unmistakably crucial component, Service Control Policies (SCPs). Our Special Report digs deep into the nitty-gritty of AWS Organizations SCP Enforcement Troubleshooting. It's a comprehensive resource designed not only to declutter the complexities but also to equip you with practical troubleshooting strategies. Despite being intense in its technical nature, we assure you that this report is crafted to be pragmatically digestible, simplifying the intricate world of AWS Organizations' SCP and its enforcement issues to ease the strain on your professional life. Crystalize your understanding of AWS, refine your problem-approaching tactics, and grow your tech-savviness with our Special Report. Step into the practical realm of cloud computing control, and decrypt AWS like never before. Here's to meaningful learning and more efficient, less stressful troubleshooting!

Chapter 2. Understanding AWS Organizations and Service Control Policies

In order to comprehend the intricacies of AWS Organizations and Service Control Policies (SCPs), it is vital to first establish a solid foundation. This section dives into the world of AWS Organizations and the pivotal role of SCPs, ensuring you grasp these often-complex components of cloud computing.

AWS Organizations is a cloud service offered by Amazon Web Services. It's designed for managing multiple AWS accounts within a single entity, known as an organization. This group of accounts typically represents a business, allowing greater control over billing, access control, and shared resources.

2.1. AWS Organizations: A Closer Look

AWS Organizations provides robust, policy-based management for multiple AWS accounts. In AWS Organizations, you can create member accounts and invite existing accounts to join your organization. Think of an AWS Organization as a tree structure, with the master account at the root, and OU (Organizational Units) as branches stemming out.

It allows you to apply various control policies, both at the organization level as well as at the OU level. Policies can also be fine-tuned for specific accounts. AWS Organizations provides flexibility and control, letting you structure your organization's accounts and resources in a way that best serves your operational requirements.

By centralizing your AWS accounts, you can gain metering and billing benefits, shared resource advantages, and optimize costs. However, note that although the policy-based control mechanism provides considerable power, it also introduces complexity, especially when you are trying to troubleshoot issues related to policy enforcement. This is where Service Control Policies (SCPs) come into play.

2.2. Service Control Policies: An Introduction

Service Control Policies, or SCPs, are akin to the traffic control system of your AWS Organizations. They manage the permissions that determine which AWS service actions can be executed by entities (such as IAM users and roles, root users, etc.) within your AWS Organization's member accounts.

Here's an analogy. Think of your organization as a city, where the city council decides on the laws and regulations. The city council here represents the Service Control Policies. They have the authority to control what can and cannot be done within the city (your organization).

However, SCPs don't grant permissions but act as a permissions boundary. An SCP defines the maximum permissions that can exist within an account. They act as safeguards, letting you establish rules that prevent member accounts from violating the core principles you set, even if the member accounts grant permissions beyond the boundaries.

2.3. Structure of an SCP

An SCP is a JSON document that includes a `Version`, `Statement`, and optional `Condition` elements. The `Version` is the policy language version. The `Statement` element is where the policy's guts exist. It contains the `Principal`, `Action`, `Resource`, and `Effect` elements.

Understand that the `Effect` can be `Allow` or `Deny`. When an entity within an AWS account sends a request to an AWS service, AWS determines whether the request should be allowed or denied based on all the SCPs that apply to the account.

The `Principal` is the entity making the request, the `Action` is the action in the request, and the `Resource` is the object that the action is targeting.

2.4. Setting up and Managing SCPs

In order to manage SCPs, navigate to the AWS Organizations console and select "Policies" on the navigation pane. From this panel, you'll be able to create, edit, and manage your SCPs. A key aspect of managing SCPs efficiently is to be as granular as possible in your policies.

Setting up SCPs involves determining the necessary permissions to allow or deny, writing the JSON document policy, and attaching the policy to your organization, OUs, or specific accounts.

Remember, the SCP enforcement at the AWS account level is governed by the intersection of all SCPs applied to an account. This includes any SCPs attached to the organization root, the OU that the account is part of, and any SCPs directly attached to the account itself.

2.5. Diagnosing and Troubleshooting SCP Issues

SCP issues can originate from various sources. A common problem — an end-user not being able to perform an allowed operation — can be a direct result of SCPs blocking certain permissions. As an AWS Organization administrator, understanding how to diagnose and troubleshoot these issues is invaluable.

Tools for diagnosing include AWS IAM Policy Simulator and AWS CloudTrail. They provide insights and logging capabilities that can assist in determining why a certain AWS operation is being denied.

Remember, troubleshooting SCP issues often involve interpreting complex JSON document policies with multiple nested structures. A deep understanding of both the AWS service in question and the SCP structure itself is crucial to navigate through and troubleshoot effectively.

In summary, AWS Organizations and Service Control Policies are powerful management tools for multiple AWS accounts. They provide much-needed control and protection, but they also add layers of complexity. It's essential to take time to understand, strategize, and plan their deployment and ongoing management to reap all the benefits while minimizing any potential challenges. This understanding lays the foundation to effectively navigate the SCP enforcement troubleshooting landscape.

Chapter 3. Decoding the Intricacies of AWS Hierarchies

With a multi-account structure, AWS Organizations makes it feasible to generate a hierarchy within accounts that is centralized and easily managed. We will first illustrate the theory of AWS hierarchy before unlocking its mechanisms.

3.1. Understanding AWS Hierarchy Basics

The overarching structure of AWS Organizations is often likened to a tree, fundamentally consisting of the root, OU (Organizational Units), and member accounts.

A root is an entity at the very apex of the organization structure and contains all OUs and accounts. There is only one root per organization and it takes accountability for establishing SCP (Service Control Policies) which are applicable to all the accounts beneath it.

An OU is essentially a container within the root or other OUs, where you can manage multiple AWS accounts in a collective approach. The virtue of utilizing OUs lies in simplification and homogenization of SCPs.

Speaking about member accounts, they illustrate individual entities in AWS. An account can belong to an OU, or it could merely be linked to the root. Each AWS account under the organization can be controlled individually, while also being regulated by the SCP assigned at root and OU levels.

3.2. In-Depth into AWS Organizations Structure

A deeper look into the AWS Organizations' tree-like structure would clarify how AWS accounts and OUs are placed within the roots. The hierarchy starts with the root, followed by OUs, sub-OUs, and finally the AWS accounts.

It's beneficial to conjure the AWS hierarchy as a myriad of containers where policies can be applied. The root holds the entire organization and can apply SCPs that apply to every account in the organization. In turn, within the root, we'll find our OUs, acting as sub-containers. They can apply their own SCPs, overruling root policies if explicitly allowed to, or adding to them if they don't conflict. OUs can also contain sub-OUs, rendering an additional layer of policy manipulation.

A propagated strategy is to create OUs according to environmental similarities, i.e., production environment, development environment, and a testing environment, each with their own distinct set of policies.

3.3. Service Control Policies (SCPs) and Their Role in AWS Hierarchies

In the AWS hierarchy, SCPs play an unquestionably pivotal role. They are JSON policies that specify the maximum permissions for account users and roles, controlling what actions are allowed or denied in the AWS accounts.

The SCPs shape and control the landscape of AWS hierarchies and can be created and applied at each level - root, OUs, and individual accounts. For this to happen efficiently, an understanding of Policy Inheritance is cardinal.

3.4. AWS Policy Inheritance

In AWS Organizations, a policy at a higher level holds prevalence on the subordinate levels. This phenomenon, dubbed as policy inheritance, dictates that an applied policy at any given level in the hierarchy will impact all the levels beneath it in the hierarchy tree.

The flexibility offered by this inheritance model is notable. Although the policies set at the root influence all member OUs and accounts, a different SCP can be applied to individual OUs to make their rules more restrictive or specific, overruling root level policies where required.

Furthermore, sub-OUs can further tighten or specify the policies as per their needs. However, it is key to remember that a policy can never grant more permissions than its parent, i.e. an SCP applied at an OU or account level cannot override the restrictions enforced by the SCP at the root.

This exploration of AWS hierarchies serves as a map to navigate the seemingly complicated landscape of AWS Organizations. By understanding the fundamental building blocks and how they interact with each other, you can effectively strategize, customize, and navigate your AWS environment, making your cloud computing journey both efficient and empowering. Each OU, sub-OU, and policy forms a crucial part to solve the puzzle of AWS hierarchy. Armed with this knowledge, you are ready to dive deeper into the ocean of AWS management, weaving complexity into productivity like never before.

Chapter 4. Diving into AWS Organizations' Multi-account Structures

In the world of AWS Organizations, managing multi-account structures is foundational. The need for different AWS accounts stems from varied user requirements, such as security, billing, and resource management.

4.1. Understanding AWS Organizations

AWS Organizations is a service that allows you to centralize governance across multiple AWS accounts. It allows you to organize accounts into groups, set fine-tuned permissions, and automate AWS account creation and management.

A typical AWS Organization has a single management account and any number of member accounts. The management account has vast powers, being able to create other accounts and wholeheartedly dictate their permissions. To segregate responsibilities, member accounts are usually controlled by different teams within an organization.

AWS Organizations provides consolidated billing, meaning all AWS accounts' usage is combined, effectively giving volume discounts to all services, even if they run separately.

4.2. Navigating Multi-account Structures

Creating multiple accounts within AWS Organizations is a straightforward process, particularly when you understand the reasons for having different accounts.

Firstly, different accounts provide an excellent way of ensuring complete resource isolation. Each account has its own resources that are separate from other accounts. This is beneficial in scenarios where absolute isolation of resources and processes is crucial – for example, in production, development, and testing environments.

Second, accounts support different levels of access control and permissions. You can have a set of users accessing resources in one account, and another set of users accessing resources in another, promoting the segregation of duties.

Creating separate accounts for different layers of service can be beneficial. It's easier to monitor, manage, and track resources within a specific account rather than sifting through combined resources of multiple services.

Finally, important account-related limits are applicable at an individual account level. Having multiple accounts helps overcome some limits posed by AWS.

4.3. Setting Up Organizational Units

An Organizational Unit (OU) in AWS Organizations is a way to group accounts with similar needs, issues, or use cases. Every AWS Organization has a root that can contain multiple OUs, with every OU potentially containing multiple accounts or OUs. This structure serves to create a potential hierarchy of OUs and accounts, tailored according to specific organizational needs.

Creating an OU is a simple process achieved via the AWS Management Console or by using the AWS CLI or SDKs. Once created, you can invite existing AWS accounts to join your organization and then move them into OUs.

To ensure effective governance, AWS lets you apply Service Control Policies (SCPs) to an OU, which trickle down to all accounts within the OU. These policies define what services and actions users, roles, and permissions can use.

4.4. Leveraging Service Control Policies

Service Control Policies (SCPs) are the mechanism by which permissions are granted or denied within AWS Organizations. These JSON documents, attached to roots, OUs or individual accounts, control AWS service actions that can be performed.

To use SCPs effectively, you need to understand their structure and how they work. An SCP has an effect ("Allow" or "Deny"), a service (the AWS service that it applies to), and an action (what actions in the specified services are allowed or denied).

All accounts have an implicit full access policy by default. However, when an SCP is associated with an account, it overlays the full access policy. The SCP doesn't grant permissions. Instead, it defines the maximum permissions for an entity (like an IAM user).

In a bid to manage complexity with large organizations, AWS Organizations supports principal of least privilege by allowing multiple SCPs to be associated with an entity. The effective permissions are the result of the intersection of SCPs associated with it.

4.5. Analyzing Multi-account Strategies

Choosing an effective multi-account strategy involves analyzing different aspects of your AWS workloads, the nature of your applications, cost implications, and your enterprise security posture.

Commonly, there are three main strategies:

1. One account for all workloads.

2. One account per team or project.

3. One account per workload or application.

Your choice should be driven by your specific requirements. But remember, nothing is permanent in AWS — you can always modify your multi-account strategy to fit with the evolving needs of your organization.

4.6. Centralized Management Panel

The AWS Management Console is your one-stop location to manage your multi-account environment. You can create, invite, organize, and manage accounts and OUs. You can also define, attach, and manage SCPs.

Through AWS CloudTrail integration, AWS Organizations also provides a comprehensive view of the activities within your organization, helping you maintain control over AWS service actions carried out within your accounts.

4.7. Conclusion

Diving into AWS Organizations' multi-account structures might seem like a daunting task, but with a clear understanding and systematic approach, managing these structures can become a doable task. In the subsequent chapters, we will delve deeper into topics like SCPs, effective strategies, and tips for troubleshooting issues, thus reshaping your journey with AWS Organizations.

Chapter 5. Essentials of Service Control Policies (SCPs)

Service Control Policies (SCPs) are pivotal to managing and securing your AWS accounts. They provide governance and set boundaries by determining what actions can be performed in the accounts they are assigned to.

In order to fully comprehend the relevance and operation of SCPs, this section delves into understanding their integral concepts, functions, and best usage practices. Absorb the depth of knowledge that this section avails to remove any ambiguities around SCPs.

5.1. Understanding Service Control Policies

At the very beginning, it is crucial to understand what SCPs are, and to clear any confusion, they are NOT Identity and Access Management (IAM) policies. While IAM policies govern what actions AWS users and roles can perform, SCPs are directly tied to the AWS Organization.

Service Control Policies are applied to an organization unit (OU), root, or individual AWS accounts. SCPs regulate what services and specific actions the entities they are attached to can access, acting as a safeguard against unexpected or unauthorized resource allocation. They essentially form a 'whitelisting' or 'blacklisting' operation.

It's important to note that SCPs don't grant permissions, but restrict them. Hence, removing an SCP can never grant more access to a user.

5.2. Typical Use Cases of SCPs

The application of SCPs can be diverse and expansive, depending on the unique requirements of an organization. Here are a few typical use-cases:

1. Restricted Access: A common use case of SCPs is to prevent entities within an organization from gaining access to certain AWS services.

2. Cost Management: SCPs can be employed to block the provisioning of expensive resources, thereby helping control the budget.

3. Security: To ensure robust security, SCPs can be used to deny actions that could pose a risk, such as deleting important IAM roles or disabling CloudTrail.

5.3. Creation and Implementation of SCPs

When it comes to creating and implementing SCPs, administrators should give attention to their organization structure. The organization structure, consisting of OUs, accounts, and the root, must be aptly leveraged to apply the right policy at the right place.

To create an SCP, navigate to the AWS Organizations page, choose 'Policies' from the navigation pane, and then 'Service Control Policies'. After providing a name and description, administrators can define the policy in JSON format.

Implementing an SCP is a three-step process. First, the SCP is created. Then, it is attached to the root, an OU, or an AWS account. Finally, the respective IAM policies are adjusted.

Here's a simplified outline:

1. Create the SCP.

2. Attach the SCP to the right AWS artifact.

3. Adjust IAM policies if needed.

5.4. Strategies for using SCPs Efficiently

SCPs, if used correctly, can be a powerful tool in managing your AWS resources effectively. However, you should be cautious while using them as inappropriate implementation might result in unexpected access restrictions.

1. Apply the Principle of Least Privilege: Always create SCPs keeping the least privilege model in mind.

2. Regularly Monitor: Regularly check the efficiency of your SCPs and make modifications if necessary.

3. Layer Your Policies: Are some parts of your AWS Organization needing broader access while others need to be tightly controlled? Layer your policies accordingly.

4. Use AWS Managed Policies: AWS provides some pre-configured managed policies. Use them as a starting point in your SCP creation process.

5.5. Common Troubleshooting Strategies for SCPs

Things could go wrong while using SCPs, but the key is to know the possible solutions. Here are some common troubleshooting strategies:

1. Check If Necessary Services Are Allowed: Sometimes, certain services might not work due to SCPs blocking necessary services

related to those. To fix this, identify the missing services and include them in your SCPs.

2. Examine IAM Policies: If an SCP is blocking a service it should not, re-examine your IAM policies. Remember that the outcome is a resultant of both IAM and SCPs policies.

3. Review Deny Statements: Start troubleshooting your issues with the deny statements. If you see an 'implicitDeny' error, consider checking the SCPs first as IAM policies do not have implicit deny.

5.6. Conclusion

In summing up, SCPs offer a broad surface for refining control over AWS services and resources. Ensuring their proper use can save an organization from unexpected encounters and, in fact, strengthen the cloud security posture.

Just as importantly, traversing the path of identifying and implementing the right SCPs inculcates a mindset that pushes for growth and understanding within AWS' vast offering. Understanding these facets will help you construct a more solid foundation, ready to absorb advanced subjects with clarity and perspective.

Chapter 6. SCP Enforcement: Processes and Mechanisms

The engine that drives AWS Organizations is Service Control Policies (SCPs). SCPs blend the essential aspects of permission control and account management, ensuring the secure and compliant use of AWS resources across multiple accounts. Ensuring that SCPs function smoothly is an enforcement process that needs understanding and meticulousness to manage effectively. This section delves into this process, revealing the mechanisms at work behind every enforcement action.

6.1. Understanding the importance of SCPs

SCPs are, in essence, the DNA of AWS Organizations. In terms of security and compliance, these policies are built to influence and control how specific AWS services and actions are used across different accounts within an organization. They essentially define the maximum permissions that IAM principals (which could be users or roles) can have when it comes to specific AWS resources.

In an AWS environment, an SCP evaluates every interaction, determining whether it falls within the pre-defined compliance and permissions guidelines. Only when an action aligns with the expectations outlined within the active SCPs is it allowed to proceed. This process highlights the importance of having SCPs properly set up.

You must be aware that SCPs are not standalone measures. They work together with IAM policies, complementing and enhancing the control measures to ensure more secure account activity.

6.2. How SCPs Work

SCPs are profoundly interconnected with the structure of the AWS Organizations that they reside in. They can be directly attached to any of the organization's roots, organizational units (OUs), or accounts.

Once an SCP is associated with a root, it will automatically apply to every OU and account under that root unless otherwise specified by another SCP. In the case of OUs, the SCP would apply to that OU and its contents, down to the nested OUs and respective accounts.

The intersection of the policies applied to an entity from its roots all the way to its units is what defines the maximum permissions of the IAM principals.

SCPs follow a 'deny by default' model similar to IAM policies. If you don't explicitly allow an action in your SCP, it's implicitly denied.

And remember, SCPs do not grant permissions; they filter the permissions that are attached to IAM entities. So, if a certain permission is not allotted to an IAM principal via IAM policies, mentioning that in an SCP will not grant the IAM principal that permission.

6.3. SCP Enforcement and Troubleshooting

When it comes to SCP enforcement, one should understand that many factors can influence the operational aspects of the enforcement process. The practical procedure of SCP enforcement is not a linear process; it constitutes checking the entire tree of policies attached to an entity at all levels. Here, we will delve into how you can anticipate and troubleshoot problems associated with SCP enforcement.

The first step when troubleshooting is to understand the relationship between SCPs and IAM policies. SCP enforcement by AWS is dependent on multiple factors, both within SCPs and IAM policies. The permissions given in IAM roles/users/groups and the conditions placed in SCPs all contribute to the final permissions a principal has.

One common issue that arises during SCP enforcement is blanket denial or allowance of actions that should not be. This often results from too broad a permission given in IAM roles/users/groups and too tight or relaxed conditions in SCPs. When SCP enforcement results in unexpected permission sets, checking the above could prove the root cause.

Another common issue is when users are unsure of the SCPs that are affecting their permissions. AWS provides an IAM policy simulator that can help you simulate and understand the policies at work, thus aiding in identifying more obscure problems.

Understanding the AWS IAM policy evaluation logic is another key thing crucial when troubleshooting SCP enforcement. Some critical points to note include:

- SCPs do not grant permissions; only IAM policies do so.

- SCPs placed at higher levels (closer to root) can override those at lower levels. Hence, always ensure your permissions at higher levels are set correctly and do not unintentionally override others.

- Permissions with explicit Deny will always deny regardless of any Allows that may exist.

Understanding and mastering SCP enforcement processes and mechanisms is undoubtedly challenging. However, the potential for increased control, security, and efficiency that comes with it far outweighs the initial struggle. Armed with a deep understanding of SCPs and their nuances, you can efficiently manage and troubleshoot your ever-evolving AWS environment.

Chapter 7. Troubleshooting Common SCP Challenges

Understanding AWS Organizations' Service Control Policies (SCPs) and troubleshooting their common challenges necessitate an intricate knowledge of the system. Our strategy here is to unravel this journey into more manageable sections that pinpoint key aspects of SCP troubleshooting. By so doing, we provide a tool that not only helps you tackle your cloud computing problems but enables you to become more proficient and confident in navigating the AWS environment.

7.1. Understanding SCPs

Cloud computing in AWS involves many resources and accounts, which often lead to a multi-layered, intricate landscape. The introduction of SCPs significantly shifted this landscape. SCPs function as a determining factor for the AWS services and actions acquirable by your IAM users and roles. They bring order and discipline to account relations by allowing you to define levels of access across your AWS organization.

When setting SCPs, keep in mind that denying access to a service or action holds higher precedence over any allowances defined elsewhere in your IAM policies. Therefore, before you blame SCPs for a problem, confirm that the service you're trying to access isn't denied in any of your SCPs.

7.2. Common SCP Challenges and Their Solutions

7.2.1. Challenge 1: Services Inaccessible Despite Policies

Many users run into scenarios where, despite having affirmed the requisite policies, some services remain inaccessible. In most cases, this problem emanates from the SCP denying access. For example, imagine you have an SCP denying access to the Relational Database Service (RDS). Even if an IAM policy allows RDS, the users won't be able to access it owing to the SCP's precedence.

To rectify this, check the SCPs linked to your entity. If any of them contain explicit Deny actions on RDS, then that's probably the culprit. Alter or subtract those policies to restore service access.

7.2.2. Challenge 2: Roles Having Overreaching Permissions

Sometimes, you may find that some IAM roles hold more permissions than desired. Investigate your policies and see if they have statement-less SCPs. The absence of an explicit deny in an SCP will take into account the IAM policies, which could allow too many services.

Modify these policies to include a more granular level of permissions - specifically, what you wish these roles to access.

7.2.3. Challenge 3: Confusion While Handling Multiple Accounts

AWS Organizations allows for the creation of multiple accounts, and with many accounts come complexity. You may find it problematic to track which policies are active where.

To mitigate this issue, utilize tagging for policies. AWS supports adding tags to policies, making them readily identifiable. Keep your tags descriptive to manage and understand your policies better.

7.2.4. Challenge 4: Unexpected Denies

IAM policies can become a sticking point when it comes to fine-tuning permissions by using condition keys, especially when combined with SCPs. If you have an SCP with a condition (let's say on "AWS:RequestedRegion") and a user tries to perform an action outside the defined condition, AWS denies the action, leading to unexpected denies.

The key to solving this lies in the policy language. Review your conditions and ensure they reflect your actual requirements correctly.

7.3. Advance Troubleshooting Techniques

Moving a notch higher, let's examine some advanced troubleshooting techniques. These methods primarily revolve around reviewing logs, tracing requests, making sense of error messages, and understanding SCP evaluation logic.

AWS CloudTrail provides an excellent way to monitor your account's actions, including policies. Any changes made to policies, including additions, deletions, and modifications, are logged in here.

AWS IAM Access Analyzer helps you identify resources within your organization and accounts that are shared with an entity outside of it. It generates a detailed report of all the accessed policies and any conditions there maybe.

These resources contribute significantly to the understanding of SCPs, as well as addressing more complex issues you might encounter. They demystify the policies landscape, open up fresh problem-approaching techniques, and help you weave through the complexity of cloud computing in AWS.

Troubleshooting SCPs can be daunting, but the right approach, combined with the right tools, can make a world of difference. Pore over your IAM policies, understand your SCPs, make use of the available AWS resources. The goal here is to turn a formidable challenge into a seamless experience.

By breaking the problems down, understanding them, and approaching them logically, you can decrypt the AWS cloud computing conundrum with relative ease and confidence. Learning to troubleshoot SCP enforcement issues is an imperative skill in this era of cloud computing. It lessens the stress of managing your cloud computing resources and capacitates you to troubleshoot efficiently—equipping you for a smoother journey in the AWS Organizations world.

Chapter 8. Delving into Advanced SCP Enforcement Issues

In the exploration of Service Control Policies' (SCPs) enforcement issues, a suite of advanced challenges might arise. This deep dive into these issues lends you the knowledge necessary for identifying, understanding, and troubleshooting them effectively. We start our journey by looking at conflicting SCPs, circling around the examination of permission boundaries, and concluding with diagnosing surprising results.

8.1. Addressing Conflicting SCPs

One of the most common challenges faced by administrators when managing SCPs is dealing with conflicting policies. This usually happens when an SCP denies an action that another policy explicitly allows.

SCP conflicts can significantly derail the operational flow. Therefore, identifying and resolving these conflicts quickly is vital for the effective functioning of an AWS Organization. SCP enforcement follows an explicit deny strategy, meaning that if even one SCP denies a particular action, the permission to execute that action is denied, irrespective of other policies.

To troubleshoot conflicting SCPs, probe the affected permissions, checking if the service that got denied permission appears in any other SCP with an explicit deny statement. Should such conflict exist, consider revising the conflicting SCPs to ensure smooth operation.

8.2. Unraveling Permission Boundaries

Permission boundaries in an IAM role pose their own unique set of challenges. A permission boundary is an advanced feature in which an administrator sets the maximum permissions that an identity-based policy can grant to an IAM entity.

If a user is unable to execute certain actions despite having the necessary permissions, the problem might lie in the attached permission boundaries. A striking feature of permission boundaries is that unlike SCPs, they do not deny service actions outright but limit the maximum permissions that can be granted.

To untangle issues related to permission boundaries, investigate to confirm if the permission boundaries are not allowing the required action for the role. Familiarize yourself with all attached IAM policies and cross-check them against the AWS managed policy that initiates the issue. This insight not only confirms if the problem starts with the permission boundaries but also helps determine the next steps, speeding the troubleshooting process.

8.3. Diagnosing Surprising Results

AWS Organizations and SCPs can sometimes yield unexpected results, leaving you with an action that should have been allowed but was denied, or vice versa. These anomalies might be due to an incorrect understanding of the policies, misleading configuration, or underlying misconfiguration in the AWS Organization.

Unforeseen results are usually a product of a misunderstanding of the multiple layers that the policy enforcement has. Be it AWS-managed policies, inline policies, or SCPs, each layer contributes to the final permission verdict. Having a good grasp of how these multiple layers interact within AWS Organizations will help you to solve these surprising outcomes.

To diagnose these unexpected instances, thoroughly evaluate each IAM User, Group, or Role that experienced an unexpected result. Look into the policies attached to these entities and their specifics. This rigorous inquiry will propel you towards the possible root of the problem. Follow this by validating all service-specific permissions. You might find that, unexpectedly, the policy does not include essential permissions for your use case.

When troubleshooting SCP enforcement issues in AWS Organizations, remember that the intersection of multiple policies and permissions result in a complex decision tree. Therefore, developing a strong understanding of AWS permissions and their enforcement policies becomes crucial. So, roll up your sleeves, delve into the world of AWS, and confront the challenges head on!

Chapter 9. Best Practice Approaches to SCP Troubleshooting

In a world where cloud complexity is only rivaled by its necessity, Service Control Policies (SCPs) stand as the bulwark of structure within AWS Organizations, often the gatekeepers of sanity in the tumultuous seas of multi-account management. Approaching SCPs is similar to tackling any complex beast—strategizing and implementing best practices is the best way forward.

9.1. Getting Started with SCP

Our journey begins with a crucial foundational step - understanding what Service Control Policies are. SCPs provide central control across an AWS organization to ensure AWS services align with your business practices. These policies are JSON documents, and they, in essence, allow or disallow permissions to the various AWS service actions available.

Getting acquainted with the JSON syntax is of utmost importance when dealing with SCPs. It's not as daunting as it might seem. Here is a simple example:

```json
{
  "Version": "2012-10-17",
  "Statement": [
    {
      "Effect": "Allow",
      "Action": "*",
      "Resource": "*"
    }
```

```
    ]
  }
```

This example allows all actions across all AWS services.

9.2. Optimizing SCP Structure

While defining SCPs, taking a broad approach isn't advisable. Permitting everything for every user can lead to a lack of control and potential security breaches, whereas a too narrow policy could limit productivity and flexibility. The best practice approach necessitates a balance between restrictiveness and empowerment – a nuanced approach to defining permissions and resources.

Consider grouping AWS services by their nature and associated tasks. Then, assign access depending on the employee role within your organization. For instance, EC2 instances, S3 buckets, and DynamoDB could be kept under data processing services, and IAM, Cognito can be classified as Identity and Access Management services.

9.3. Understanding Policy Evaluation

Policy evaluation in AWS fundamentally works on a principle of explicit denial. If a user is denied a permission in just one policy among the many attached to them, they would not have access to that action.

IAM policies, SCPs, permissions boundaries, session policies, and resource-based policies are evaluated to come up with an effective permission set, and if one of them explicitly denies a permission, then the user won't be able to make the corresponding AWS request.

Understanding this fundamental principle is essential to successful

SCP troubleshooting because denial in access often roots back to an explicit denial in any one of the several policies attached.

9.4. Taking Advantage of Policy Simulators

AWS provides tools like the IAM Policy Simulator that can be extremely useful while troubleshooting. Use simulators to debug policies. Enter the relevant policies, specify the user, role, and service actions, and the simulator can show what the effect would be - whether the operation would be allowed or denied.

9.5. Continuous Monitoring and Revision

To avoid SCP related muddles, it's best to adopt a proactive approach rather than a reactive one. Regularly review and update custom SCPs to reflect changing business needs. AWS CloudTrail logs every API call in the AWS environment and can prove crucial for flagging unexpected activities. Make frequent use of CloudWatch alarms for more efficient and accurate monitoring of the system.

We cannot overstress the paramount importance of understanding the basic principles and the broad, layered structure of policy operation for effective troubleshooting. It equips you to swiftly identify the source when things go awry and centralizes your investigation efforts effectively.

9.6. Closing Notes

Cloud computing, despite its intricacies, shouldn't be a Rorschach test of confusion. Effective strategies, knowledge of best practices, and tools, can equip one sufficiently, not just to weather the storm but to take control. AWS SCPs, while complex, promise a structured, secure, manageable framework if approached holistically.

This was a walk-through introduction to SCP troubleshooting within AWS Organization. Getting familiar with the JSON structure, strategizing SCPs, understanding policy evaluations and utilizing AWS tools go a long way to understand, prevent, and troubleshoot SCP issues. However, it's worth noting that mastering SCP troubleshooting is a continuous learning process that requires time and patience.

Stay curious. Stay informed. Decode the mysteries of AWS like never before.

Chapter 10. Case Studies: Real-world SCP Enforcement Scenarios

In the world of AWS, Service Control Policies (SCPs) play a fundamental role, acting as the guardians of your cloud network. Enforced at various points of the AWS Organizations' hierarchy, they serve to define the boundaries for an organization and its subsequent entities. However, troubleshooting SCP enforcement scenarios might be quite a handful, especially without comprehensive real-world examples to guide you through. Here, we will explore a series of case studies drawn from actual SCP enforcement situations.

10.1. Case Study 1: Unexpected Denial of Access in an Organizational Unit

Imagine you're in an organization where the Root has an SCP allowing all services except for Amazon EC2. An Organizational Unit (OU) nested under this Root, incidentally, has another SCP, explicitly allowing Amazon EC2 with selected actions.

Post deployment of these policies, there's a bout of confusion as members find themselves abruptly denied access to Amazon EC2 services, contrary to the expectation. Here lies an often misunderstood aspect of AWS Organizations—SCPs enforce the principle of least privilege. That implies that all permissions are independently evaluated for the intersecting set. So, even though the OU has an SCP allowing Amazon EC2, the SCP at the Root, which blocks Amazon EC2, supersedes and results in the denial.

Should you find yourself in an analogous situation, revisit and align your SCPs to avoid conflicts—creating harmony between your Root and OU level SCPs.

10.2. Case Study 2: Inadequate IAM user permissions

Consider an AWS organization where you, as a security administrator, have established SCPs and are adequately restricting service access across the hierarchy. Unfortunately, users within an OU start reporting restricted access to the AWS Management Console. This scenario raises the possibility of overlooking the IAM user permissions while focusing on SCP enforcement.

Recall that SCPs work in conjunction with IAM user permissions and access is granted following the principle of least privilege. If IAM user permissions aren't expansive enough—or worse, nonexistent—the SCP's allowances go in vain.

To troubleshoot such occurrences, ensure your IAM roles, users, and groups are correctly configured with sufficient permissions. It's essentially about striking a balance between SCP's enforcement and IAM's user-level access control.

10.3. Case Study 3: CloudTrail logs not capturing SCP changes

Now picture a scenario where an organization diligently monitors AWS CloudTrail for operations and account activity tracking. However, you notice SCP changes at the OU level are not being logged, hindering your organization's audit trail.

CloudTrail's service event history includes actions from AWS Management Console, AWS SDKs, command line tools, and other

AWS services. However, it does not include all API actions, which might be the cause of missing SCP changes.

In such cases, use CloudWatch Events or EventBridge to log these missing operations, making the monitoring more exhaustive.

10.4. Case Study 4: Inherited SCPs causing unexpected restrictions

A final case study involves an organization operationalizing multiple OUs—with some OUs nested under others. If SCPs applied at a higher level are unexpectedly restricting actions further down the hierarchy, it may be due to SCP inheritance.

SCP permissions are effectively inherited from the Root to the last nested OU. Therefore, an SCP denying an action at a higher level will also deny that action at every subsequent level. This inheritance can often lead to unintended restrictions.

To resolve these issues, consider the inheritance hierarchy when setting SCP policies. Understanding the scope of SCP enforcement and planning ahead can reduce inadvertent permission inheritance.

These case studies show that inherent complications in SCP enforcement are manageable with appropriate knowledge and tactics. An informed approach to AWS is essential for keeping your cloud computing experience smooth and secure. Following these practical examples, the labyrinth of SCP enforcement should now be navigated with more confidence and less stress. Remember, the tool is only as good as its wielder, so continue learning and adapting to effectively utilize AWS Organizations and its SCP enforcement.

Chapter 11. Looking Ahead: Future practices in SCP Enforcement and Troubleshooting

As you embark on the journey to mastering service control policies (SCPs) and their enforcement within AWS Organizations, it is vital to keep your sights set on the horizon. This section will delve into the future practices of SCP Enforcement and Troubleshooting by exploring next-generation tools and methods, systematic best practices, and emerging tech trends.

11.1. Streamlining with Automation

The coming age will see the automation of many tasks related to SCP enforcement and troubleshooting. This is primarily due to the fast-paced development of artificial intelligence (AI) and machine learning (ML) tools. The AWS Management and Governance suite is also regularly updated with automation solutions.

For instance, AWS' CloudFormation provides methods to bring automation right into the AWS Organizations space. This allows for the templating and stacking of accounts, enabling automated setup of log archives, directories, networks, roles and SCP's among others.

It is essential, going forward, to be continually vigilant for advancements in automation, not only within the AWS ecosystem but also from third-party suppliers.

11.2. Embrace Machine Learning and AI in Troubleshooting

As hinted above, AI and ML are showing great potential in emergency troubleshooting. Consider Amazon Macie for example, a security service that employs machine learning to help identify and protect sensitive data. Macie is capable of recognizing patterns and detecting anomalies which are humanly impossible to perform with speed and accuracy; it automates the process of determining and controlling access to data, a function previously handled manually.

These AI/ML services, as they continue developing, will further simplify the SCP enforcement and troubleshooting, reducing the manual workload and increasing the speed of response.

11.3. Leveraging AWS Control Tower

AWS Control Tower provides the easiest way to set up and govern a new, secure multi-account AWS environment based on AWS best practices. For organizations with existing AWS accounts, AWS Control Tower provides the option to bring those accounts into the AWS Control Tower environment. This environment's native integration with AWS Organizations and SCPs assures enhanced troubleshooting capabilities.

Going forward, AWS Control Tower is expected to incorporate more sophisticated automation, AI, and ML technology to improve the efficiency of SCP enforcement and troubleshoot more effectively.

11.4. Novel Strategies in SCP Design

Rethinking your approach to SCPs design is another key to the future. The Fine-Grained Permissions Model, for instance, is a strategy that experts say will be popular in the near future.

This model focuses on assigning permissions at a granular level; instead of giving blanket permissions to entire teams or services, give specific permissions to specific individuals or smaller teams. This technique reduces the risk of unauthorized access and makes troubleshooting easier as there are fewer variables to consider.

11.5. The Rise of Serverless Computing

AWS Lambda, a serverless computing service, is expected to play a big role in SCP enforcement and troubleshooting. As the service runs your code without provisioning or managing servers, it promises an environment where you can run your SCPs with almost no system-level worries.

Moreover, more serverless services are expected to come on board, and being on top of these developments will be key to staying ahead of the curve.

The future of SCP enforcement and troubleshooting in AWS Organizations is not without challenges, but with the right tools, strategies, and foresight, the path becomes easier. Technological developments like automation, AI, and ML will undeniably boost efficiency. The emergence of new strategies in SCP design and increasing reliance on serverless computing will also transform the way we approach enforcement and troubleshooting. Adaptation and forward-thinking are crucial as we embrace the future.